YOSEMITE
NATIONAL PARK

by Ruth Radlauer

**Design and photographs
by Rolf Zillmer**

AN ELK GROVE BOOK

 CHILDRENS PRESS®

CHICAGO

Bequest of Beauty

A bequest is a gift for those who follow. Each National Park is a BEQUEST OF BEAUTY. It is a place of special interest or beauty that has been saved by the United States government especially for you, your children, and their great-great-grandchildren. This bequest is yours to have and to care for so that others who follow can do the same during their lives.

Cover—American Elm and Half Dome

With special thanks to Craig D. Bates, Indian Cultural Program Supervisor

Library of Congress Cataloging in Publication Data
Radlauer, Ruth Shaw.
  Yosemite National Park.
  (National parks, bequest of beauty series)
  "An Elk Grove book."
  SUMMARY: Simple text and photographs introduce Yosemite National Park.
  1. Yosemite National Park—Juvenile literature.
[1. Yosemite National Park. 2. National parks and reserves] I. Zillmer, Rolf, ill. II. Title. III. Series.
F868.Y6R32   917.94'47'045   75-2160
ISBN 0-516-07486-5

Revised Edition © 1984
by Regensteiner Publishing Enterprises, Inc.
Original Copyright © 1975
by Regensteiner Publishing Enterprises, Inc.
All rights reserved. Published simultaneously in Canada.
Printed in the United States of America.

8 9 10 11 12 13 14 15 R 90

Contents

What is Yosemite National Park?

Yosemite National Park is many things. It's huge granite rocks like Half Dome, a rock that asks to be climbed. It is a lone pine tree bent and twisted by the wind that blows across the top of Sentinel Dome.

Yosemite is Mattie Lake at sunset.

It's mule deer among the leaves and black bears, squirrels, butterflies, white-headed woodpeckers, mountain lions, and porcupines.

Yosemite National Park is trees like the sugar pine, douglas fir, and the giant sequoia. It's aspen, oak, and maple trees that lose their autumn leaves before the winter sleep.

This park is the taste of icy spring water and the smell of damp ferns, the feel of soft moss on a rock, or the roar of Nevada Fall. It's hotels and camping places, hiking and skiing, horse rides and ranger talks. And it will probably be even more than these when you visit Yosemite National Park.

Mattie Lake

Half Dome

Jeffrey Pine on Sentinel Dome

Mule Deer

Nevada Fall

Where is Yosemite National Park?

Yosemite National Park is in the Sierra Nevada mountain range that runs north and south through California.

There are many ways to get there. If you leave from Reno, Nevada, you'll be in Yosemite in about 5 hours. People who drive from Los Angeles, California, need 7 hours for the trip.

From a city like New York, you can get to the area by airplane in 5 hours or by car in 5 days. If you come by airplane, you'll need a rented car or a bus ride to finish the trip.

But no matter how you travel, as soon as you get to Yosemite Valley, you'll know it's worth the trip.

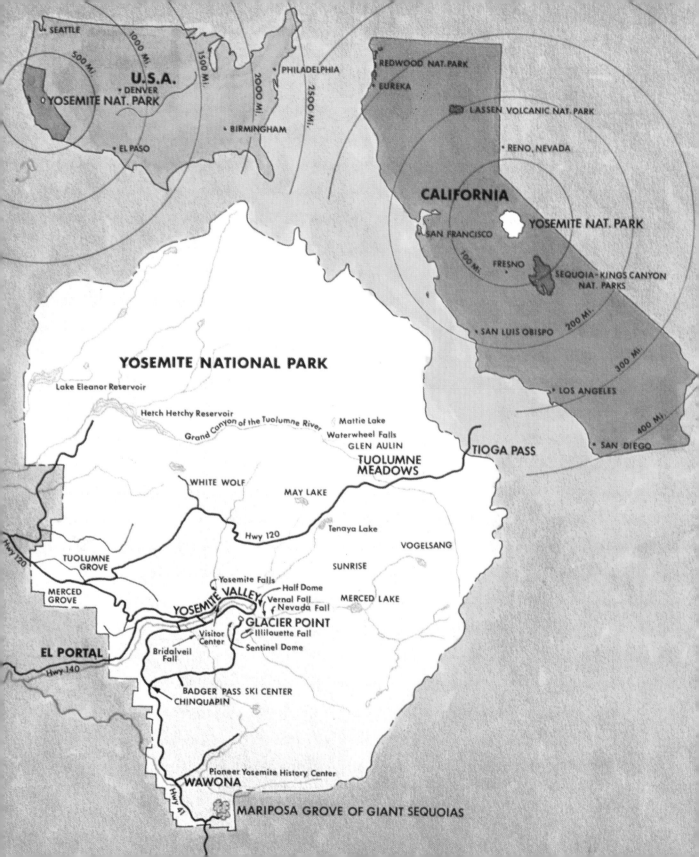

U.S.A.

SEATTLE

500 MI.
1000 MI.
1500 MI.
2000 MI.
2500 MI.

DENVER
YOSEMITE NAT. PARK

PHILADELPHIA

BIRMINGHAM

EL PASO

CALIFORNIA

REDWOOD NAT. PARK

EUREKA

LASSEN VOLCANIC NAT. PARK

RENO, NEVADA

YOSEMITE NAT. PARK

SAN FRANCISCO

100 MI.
FRESNO

SEQUOIA - KINGS CANYON NAT. PARKS

SAN LUIS OBISPO

200 MI.

LOS ANGELES

300 MI.

400 MI.

SAN DIEGO

YOSEMITE NATIONAL PARK

Lake Eleanor Reservoir

Hetch Hetchy Reservoir

Grand Canyon of the Tuolumne River

Mattie Lake

Waterwheel Falls

GLEN AULIN

TIOGA PASS

TUOLUMNE MEADOWS

WHITE WOLF

MAY LAKE

Hwy 120

Tenaya Lake

VOGELSANG

Hwy 120

TUOLUMNE GROVE

SUNRISE

MERCED GROVE

Yosemite Falls

Half Dome

YOSEMITE VALLEY

Vernal Fall

MERCED LAKE

Nevada Fall

GLACIER POINT

Visitor Center

Illilouette Fall

EL PORTAL

Bridalveil Fall

Sentinel Dome

Hwy 140

BADGER PASS SKI CENTER

CHINQUAPIN

Hwy 41

Pioneer Yosemite History Center

WAWONA

MARIPOSA GROVE OF GIANT SEQUOIAS

Parts of The Park

The park is so big that it's hard to decide where to go first. The main part is in Yosemite Valley where most people go to camp or stay in tent-cabins and lodges.

A shuttle bus will take you to many places in the Valley. You can go to the Happy Isles Nature Center and go on several hikes from there.

Another part of the park is the wildland or wilderness. With 750 miles of trails, hikers and horse riders can go almost everywhere and see glaciers, lakes, rivers, and streams.

If you like big trees you can go to the Mariposa Grove. Giant trees have been growing there for over 2500 years.

From Mariposa Grove you should take the road to Glacier Point and Washburn Point. These are good places to see the work of the glaciers, and you can see the high country, waterfalls, Half Dome, and Cloud's Rest. You'll even have an eagle's eye view of Yosemite Valley.

Shuttle Bus And Upper Yosemite Fall ▶

Visitor Centers

When you first get to any national park, you should go to the Visitor Center. Here you can get a free newspaper that lists many things for you to do in all parts of the park. You can also see a slide program that shows all about the park.

At the Visitor Center, models and pictures show how the earth changed to make Yosemite Valley's steep cliffs and waterfalls. This is the place to hear some ranger talks. The Visitor Center is where you get permits for overnight back country hikes.

Near the Yosemite Valley Visitor Center, you can walk through Indian Village. A garden around the village shows many of the plants the Indians used in the past to make their homes, baskets, food, and medicine.

At Tuolumne Meadows Visitor Center are displays about rock formations and trees. Here, too, Park Rangers give out wilderness permits and help you plan your hike.

Ranger Programs

Rangers are the people in green uniforms with hats like Smokey the Bear's. The Rangers are there to help you enjoy Yosemite.

On a short walk from the Visitor Center, a Park Ranger tells about the history of the Valley and important places to see. On a 2-hour nature hike a Ranger tells about plants and animals, what to watch for, and the safe way to hike. You can also go on a bicycle tour with a Park Ranger.

They work at night, too. They tell stories around the campfire and give slide picture programs about backpacking, forestry, and wildlife. There is even a "night prowl." During the night prowl you go out among the trees in the dark. The Ranger shows you that the dark forest is not scary. It's a beautiful place to be.

Park Ranger Tells How And Why ►

A Story in Stone

Words and pictures can only begin to show the amazing size of Yosemite Valley. Everywhere, you can look up and see the huge granite cliffs that make its walls. These granite cliffs tell a story in stone.

About 10 million years ago this was just a wide valley with a river running through. Then an earthquake changed the shape of the land. The river flowed faster, and rushing water cut a V-shaped canyon.

Three million years ago, the Ice Age began. Layers of packed snow and ice formed glaciers thousands of feet thick. These ice glaciers moved down and scraped against the canyon walls and floor. Then it was a U-shaped canyon with very steep cliffs on each side.

When the Ice Age ended, a glacier melted and formed a lake where the valley is now. In a few thousand years the lake bottom filled with sand that came down with the river. Later, much of the lake drained and left a flat valley where you can walk through meadows and watch for deer and bears.

Yosemite Valley And Top Of Half Dome ►

The First People

In the Indian Village at the Visitor Center, you can learn about the first people of Yosemite Valley. The Indians found almost everything they needed in this valley. They used acorns and other plants for food and animals for meat and skins. With grasses and willow they made baskets. An Indian house was a cone-shaped frame of poles covered with cedar bark to keep out the rain.

The first white men in the valley were soldiers. They asked the Indians the name of their tribe. The answer sounded like "Yo shay ma tay." The Indians in Yosemite today say that was not the name of the tribe. The people were saying to each other, "There are killers among them." But the soldiers named the place Yosemite and thought it meant "fullgrown bear."

The Indians called their home Ahwahnee. In sign language the leader tried to tell what Ahwahnee meant. A soldier wrote that it meant "deep grassy valley." Today the Indians say it means "a place of a big mouth."

Indian Village ▶

Pioneer History Museum

A walk over a covered bridge takes you into the past of Yosemite. In summer, people give demonstrations in the Pioneer History Museum's log houses. They pretend they are the early settlers. You can talk to them and ask questions.

At the 1860 artists' studio you find out that artists are helping tell the folks back East about this new place.

It's 1882 at Matthew Byron's two-story house, and he's worried that he may have to move. His land may be added to the park that was formed back in 1864. That was when President Lincoln signed a bill to set up the country's first public parks.

In the 1896 schoolhouse, the teacher and students may be out repairing the building or inside doing lessons on flat pieces of rock slate.

The 1896 soldier says that since Yosemite became a *National* Park in 1890, the army has stocked the lakes with fish. He says, "We've also made miles of trails."

What do you think these people would say if you told them about airplanes, television, and moon trips?

Covered Bridge

Matthew Byron's Two-story House

Schoolhouse Repair

"1896 Soldier"

Waterfalls

Yosemite has many large and small waterfalls, too many to count. Of the 10 highest waterfalls in the world, 5 are in this park. They are Yosemite Falls, Sentinel Falls, Snow Creek Falls, Ribbon Fall, and Wapama Falls.

Yosemite has waterfalls because of the steep granite cliffs and the valleys above them. High above the granite walls, streams of melting snow fall over the cliffs in foam and spray.

The falls roar loudest in spring and early summer when they are full. Above some falls, the ground holds water like a sponge and feeds the streams all summer. But the thin layer of soil on the granite above Yosemite Falls holds very little water. When the snow melts, the water runs off quickly. Yosemite Falls is the second highest waterfall in the world. But it is usually dry by the end of summer. It must wait for the winter snows and melting ice to build up its mighty beauty once more.

Yosemite Falls drops in 3 parts: the Upper Fall, the Middle Cascade, and the Lower Fall.

Yosemite Falls ►

And More Waterfalls

Climbing to the top of Vernal Fall should be part of every visit to Yosemite. With good walking shoes and a canteen of water, you can make it to the top in about an hour. From the Happy Isles Nature Center a path goes to a bridge where you can see the waterfall. Then you can take the Mist Trail up the side to the top. You can guess why you need a raincoat on the Mist Trail in the first half of summer.

Very strong hikers can go from Vernal Fall on up to Nevada Fall. If you don't want to walk that far, you can see these falls from Washburn Point on the way to Glacier Point.

An 8-mile hike from Tuolumne Meadows takes you to Waterwheel Falls. These "wheels" are made as the water rushes down the steep Tuolumne riverbed. It crashes against big granite rocks. When the water hits the rocks, it's thrown up as high as 40 feet to form waterwheels. For over a mile down the canyon, the water makes one wheel after another.

Vernal Fall

Nevada Fall

Waterwheel Falls

Big Trees

Three groves of big trees or giant sequoias stand in Yosemite. They are Merced Grove, Tuolumne Grove, and Mariposa Grove.

In Mariposa Grove you can pay for a tram ride through the grove and get off at any stop to walk the trails. The tram drivers tell about the trees, whether they are sequoias, incense-cedars, or ponderosa pines.

Many of the sequoias, or big trees, are bigger than you can imagine until you stand under one. To walk around some, you have to take 50 giant steps. These giants have lived 2 and 3 thousand years because of their bark. Sequoia bark is very thick and doesn't burn easily. Sequoias also have an acid in the sap that protects them from insects and germs.

After a sequoia is 75 years old, it makes cones that stay on the tree for years. Each cone has about 125 to 350 seeds in it. But only one or two of these thousands of seeds grow to become a tree.

The Sequoia Called Grizzly Giant

Museum in The Sequoias

Lakes

Over 300 lakes dot the map of Yosemite. There are probably hundreds more that come and go in the high country. Some are only ponds.

Lakes are formed in different ways. Some are scooped out by glaciers. Sometimes a glacier pushes earth and rocks into a pile that makes a dam. Then the glacier melts and forms a lake. Often landslides make lakes when they dam streams or rivers.

What makes a lake disappear? The stream that feeds it may go dry. More often the lake fills with sand and silt carried by the stream. Grass begins to grow on the sand. When the stream brings more soil down from the hills, the grass traps smaller bits of soil. The land builds up until a muddy marsh forms. Finally, a meadow stands where the lake used to be.

People of the National Park Service used to try to keep lakes by scooping out the sand and silt. Now they believe it's better to "let nature take its course."

Siesta Lake ►

Rivers and Streams

There are two main rivers in Yosemite National Park: the Tuolumne and the Merced. The Tuolumne River races through a canyon in the high country. You find waterwheel falls and cascades in this river. The Tuolumne River passes through the Hetch Hetchy Reservoir. In 1914, the O'Shaughnessy Dam was built to create electric power for the city of San Francisco. The reservoir behind this dam holds that city's water supply.

The Merced River flows through Yosemite Valley without a great rush. There are many parts where you can swim and wade.

Yosemite National Park has 490 miles of streams. That's home for a lot of fish!

Both rivers and streams come from rain and melting snow. Once in a while a bit of the snow doesn't melt at all and becomes part of a mountainside glacier.

Tuolumne River

Merced River In Yosemite Valley

Merced River

A Trip in the High Country

You can see some of the lakes, rivers, and streams when you go to Tuolumne Meadows in a car. But the best way to enjoy the back country is on a pack trip with mules or by backpacking.

If you are just learning to backpack, you can get help from a Park Ranger. Rangers show visitors the kind of equipment they need for camping.

The Ranger can tell you the rules to follow to keep the wilderness good for everyone. He or she can show you how to keep warm in a snowstorm and how to choose a cooking stove.

No matter where you plan to backpack, the best place to start is at the Visitor Center in the Valley or at Tuolumne Meadows. This is where you get a Wilderness Permit. A Ranger goes over your planned trip with you. If too many people are going to the same area, the Ranger may tell you a better place to go.

Ask for a check list to make sure you have everything. Then have a good trip and leave nothing but footprints in the back country.

Backpackers ▶

Grasses, Ferns, and Flowers

When you hike in the back country, you'll see many plants. Different ones grow at different heights or elevations.

Grasses grow at low elevations in meadows. The Indians used bear grass leaf fibers to make cloth and bunch grass to make baskets. They used fern roots to make designs in the baskets.

In high wet meadows and bogs you find the small tiger lily that sometimes grows very tall. The Bigelow sneezeweed grows in low and high meadows. It may or may not make you say "Kachoo."

On the edge of melting snow banks you may come upon a snow plant. It pops up through fallen pine needles because it lives on the decaying wood and needles underneath.

In late summer, the only people who get to see the Sierra primrose are hikers. They must go to very high elevations, over 8000 feet, where it grows among granite rocks.

Bear Grass

Small Tiger Lilly

Bigelow Sneezeweed

Snow Plant

Sierra Primrose

Animals in the Park - Mammals

When you hike in the back country, you spend a lot of time in a game called, "Keep the food away from the animals."

In the Valley, Rangers play another game called "Keep the people from feeding the animals."

When you feed a squirrel peanuts and bread, he gets fat. He needs fat to keep warm in the winter, but the fat his body makes from peanuts and bread will not keep him warm. He should eat the seeds of grasses and herbs and sometimes bulbs and acorns.

The deer in Yosemite eat grass and other plants, all called browse. If you feed a deer bread, you may make it sick. People food makes a deer's stomach and insides unable to digest the browse it is meant to eat.

The black bears in the park can be dangerous, but people may be dangerous to bears. If people feed them, the bears can forget how to feed themselves. Bears hunt for food all summer and sleep most of the winter in hollow trees and caves.

Gray Squirrel

Black Bear

Mule Deer ▼

Insects,
Birds,
and Fish

And speaking of games, "Shoo the mosquito" is a big game in spring and early summer. But mosquitoes are part of the animal world. Bats and dragon flies eat them. Fish eat mosquitoes and mosquito larvae on quiet lakes.

In the Mariposa Grove you'll see many birds, especially if you leave the tram at one of the stops. Walk quietly and look carefully for any one of 30 kinds of birds here. There are western robins, Oregon juncos, white-headed woodpeckers, and the Sierra creeper.

Clark's nutcracker is a bold bird that will come close to campers. This bird eats mostly pine seeds, but also insects, larvae, and tiny mammals.

People used to "plant" fish in the rivers and streams of Yosemite. For a while they dropped tiny fish the size of your fingers into the lakes from an airplane.

Now you can fish year-round in the back country. Some of the fish include Sacramento suckers, hardhead minnow, and five kinds of trout.

Clark's Nutcracker

Mountain Climbing

You can learn some rock climbing from the Park Rangers at Yosemite. But if you really plan to become a climber, you can pay for lessons at the Yosemite Mountaineering School. In the first or basic class you learn about equipment and correct hand and foot holds. You learn to climb as high as 80 feet with the help of ropes, tools, and other climbers. You'll learn something else that's important—how to get back down.

After basic class, a mountain climber can go into another, harder class. Then he or she is ready to climb with a guide. If you don't feel that brave, you can climb the back of Half Dome with a lot of help. On the back "shoulder" of Half Dome there are cables that help you reach the top. All you do is take a deep breath, hold the cables, and start climbing, one foot after the other. It's not too hard if you take your time and a lot of deep breaths. When you see the view from up there, almost 5000 feet above the Valley floor, you'll know why people climb mountains.

Park Ranger Shows Tools

Cables Help You Climb Half Dome

Park Ranger Shows Use Of Rope

Sports

Another sport that's fun in Yosemite is horseback riding. In the summer you can rent a horse at the stables in Yosemite Valley and ride two hours, half a day, or all day.

If you want to ride out of the valley, you must have a guide. From the Valley stables, you can take a guided mule trip to Glacier Point or to Half Dome by way of Vernal Fall.

From Tuolumne Meadows Stables, you can take a 2-hour trip or a half-day ride. You can ride all day going to and from Waterwheel Falls.

If swimming is your sport, there are swimming pools at Curry Village and Yosemite Lodge.

Parts of the Merced River are deep enough for swimming, and it's a good place to row a rubber boat. Sometimes the water is very cold, so toe-testing might be a good idea.

See Yosemite On A Horse

When The Merced Is Calm, Waterplay Is Safe

Merced River Fun

Winter in the Park

Winter doesn't stop sports in Yosemite National Park. At an outdoor rink in the Valley near Camp Curry, you can go ice skating, day or night. In deepest winter the rink is banked high with snow all around.

Skiers find 6 to 12 feet of snow pack on ski slopes at Badger Pass. Lifts are there to take you up so you can ski back down. Badger Pass has good slopes for beginners as well as experts.

Ski touring goes across country. You can ski to Glacier Point and back. Very good skiers can go to the hut at Ostrander Lake in the back country.

Some people make a sport out of hunting with a camera during the winter. This is the time of year that the valley and high country put on a different display of beauty.

Learn To Ski Cross-Country

Merced River—Yosemite Valley

Your National Park

Yosemite, one of our country's first National Parks, belongs to you. But it also belongs to your neighbor and to your friends in other states and countries.

It has been here for thousands of years. Tourists have been visiting for over 100 years, and they have made many changes, good and bad.

Now the National Park Service tries to keep the park as natural as possible. Hikers are asked not to build new fire rings and not to make new trails across meadows. Backpackers must carry their own trash out of the back country.

In some places, natural fires are allowed to burn, because we know they burned long ago. Fires kept the forest floor from getting too crowded with bushes, fallen branches, and cones.

Some lakes are stocked with fish, but most are left alone to become as they were before people came.

When you visit your park, ask yourself this question. "How can I help keep Yosemite National Park alive and beautiful, a place for people to enjoy in the years to come?"

Meadow in Yosemite Valley ▶

Other National Parks in California

LASSEN VOLCANIC NATIONAL PARK is where an active volcano erupted for about 7 years between 1914 and 1921. In 1915, thick glowing lava flowed down its sides. Now it only steams. Glacier-made lakes, hot springs, and a wildlife preserve add to this park's interest.

REDWOOD NATIONAL PARK claims the tallest tree in the world, over 367 feet high. The redwoods in this park are in the same family but a different kind from the giant sequoias in the other California National Parks. This park also offers nature walks, boating, fishing, swimming, and horse riding.

SEQUOIA-KINGS CANYON NATIONAL PARKS have deep canyons and the highest peaks of the Sierra Nevada mountain range. Among the giant sequoias are the General Grant and the General Sherman. These trees are over 3 thousand years old. Their branches are longer and thicker than the main trunks of some other kinds of trees.

Lassen Volcanic National Park

Redwood National Park

Kings Canyon National Park

Sequoia National Park

About the Author and Illustrator

Ruth Radlauer's love affair with nature and National Parks began in Wyoming where she spent her summers at camp in Casper Mountain or traveling with her family in Yellowstone National Park.

Mr. and Mrs. Radlauer, graduates of the University of California at Los Angeles, are authors of many books for young people age three to thirteen. Their subjects range from social studies to youth activities such as horse riding and motorcycles.

Photographing the National Parks is a labor of love for Rolf Zillmer and his wife Evelyn. The Zillmers get an intimate view of each park since they are backpack and wildlife enthusiasts.

A former student at Art Center College of Design in Los Angeles, Mr. Zillmer was born in New York City and now makes his home in California where he is the Art Director for Elk Grove Books.